OFF TO THE CELLAR WE GO!

A GUIDE TO EXTREME WEATHER

Nature Books for Beginners

Children's Nature Books

Have you ever looked outside and thought that maybe it might be a better decision to stay inside because of the weather? While the weather can be very intriguing, it can also be quite dangerous. In this book you will read about dangerous weather conditions. Be sure to talk to your parents and teachers about what to do in case of severe weather.

THUNDERSTORMS

Thunderstorms occur as warm, moist air rises rapidly. They can bring lightning, heavy rain, high winds, and occasionally hail. They appear every day around the Earth and can start at any time, mostly occurring during the afternoon or evening during the warmer seasons.

Thunderstorms can be extremely dangerous. People are more likely to be killed from lightning than by a tornado.

Storm Clouds, Saskatchewan Prairie, Lightning Night in Canada

LIGHTNING

Lightning occurs when a powerful bolt of electricity forms and strikes the earth with great force. For lightning to occur, high winds in the thunderstorm causes water and ice particles to hit each at a high rate of speed. This will cause a charge to build up. A positive charge is created at the top of the storm, and a negative charge is created at the bottom of the storm. When the negative charge reaches a certain point, it discharges all at once, resulting in the lightning bolt.

As objects located on the ground are positively charged as well, the lightning may often strike an object located on the ground, usually striking the tallest object. It is also attracted to metal. You will want to make sure that you are inside when during a lightning storm. Do not hold anything metal and do not stand near a tree. Do not remain in a swimming pool during a storm.

A Hurricane on Earth viewed from space.

HURRICANES

Hurricanes are large, powerful storms forming over the ocean. They can range up to 600 miles wide. They bring floods, heavy rain, high winds, and storm surges and can cause major devastation.

They typically form during the summer and fall, as the water in our ocean is warm. Hurricanes obtain their energy from this warm water, which should be at least 80 degrees Fahrenheit. The high winds result from spinning around the eye of the hurricane, which is the center.

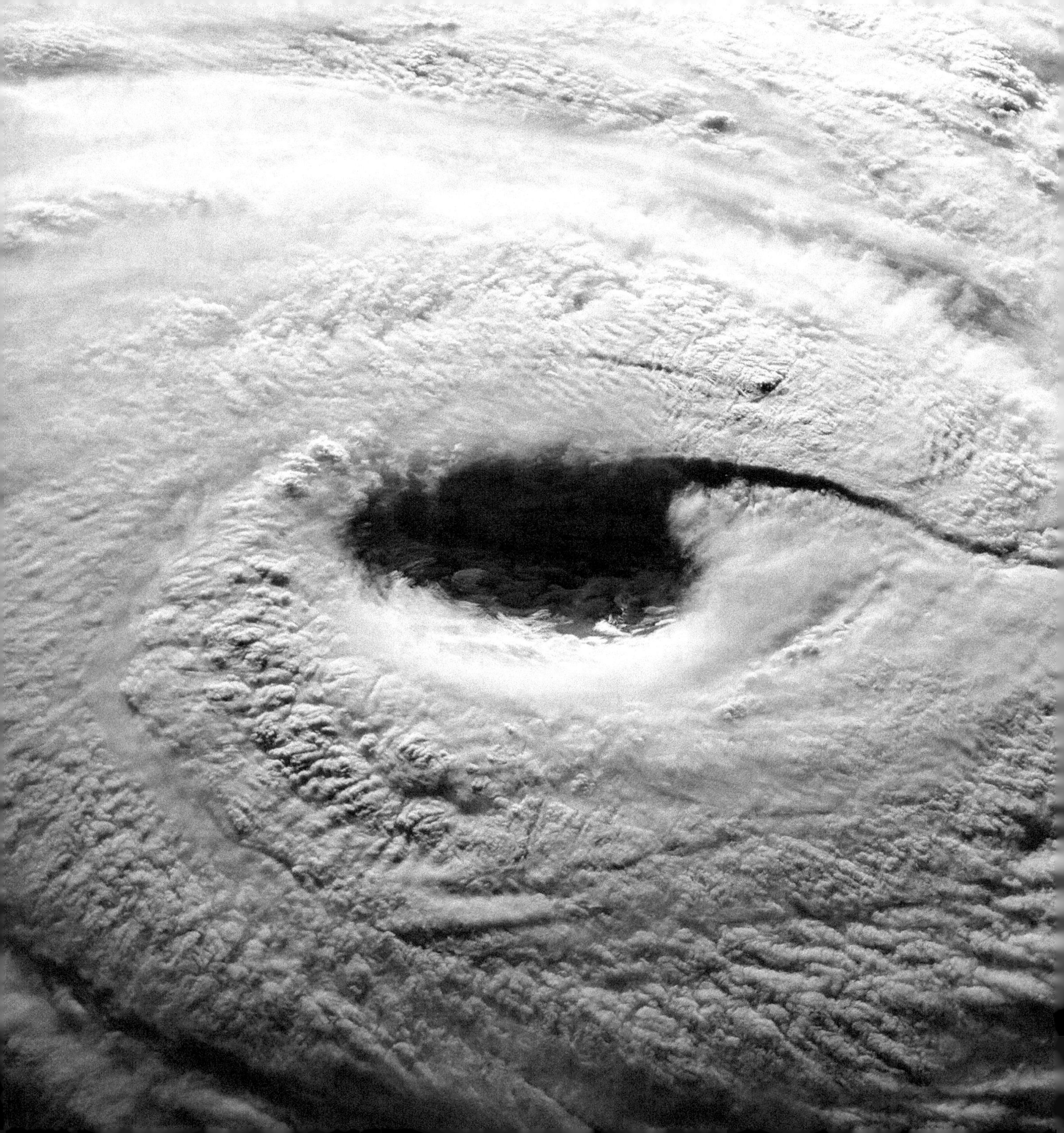

The Coriolis force of our planet's spin is what causes the spinning. At the center, the winds are usually calm, but outside of its center, winds can be steady at 80 to 150 miles per hour.

Hurricanes usually occur in certain parts of the world. They will form in the Atlantic Ocean close to the Caribbean Sea, located near the coast of Africa, as well as the Gulf of Mexico. They are referred to as Cyclones when they form in the Indian Ocean, and are known as Typhoons when they occur in the Pacific Ocean.

Typhoon over planet Earth.

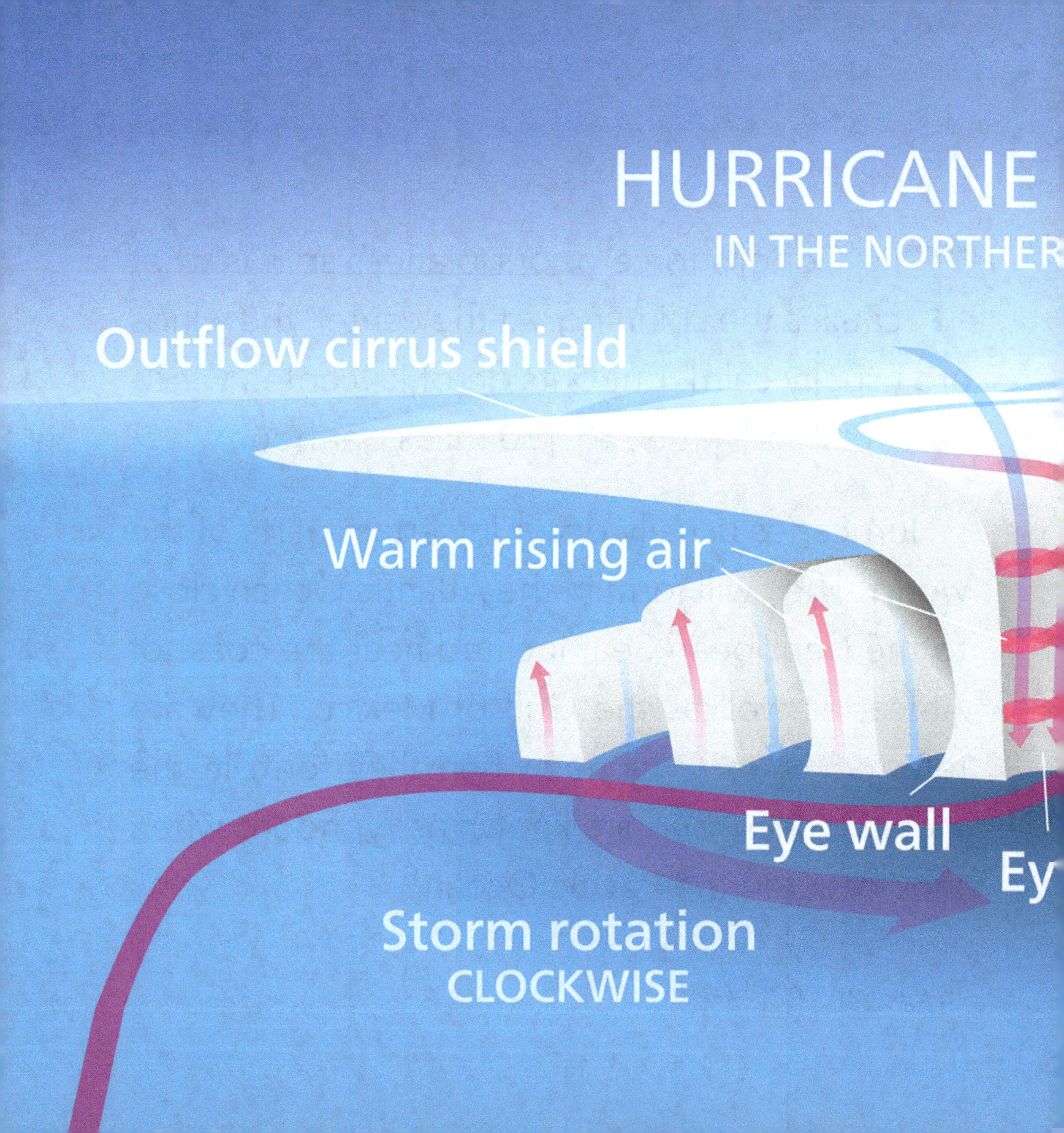

HURRICANE
IN THE NORTHER
Outflow cirrus shield
Warm rising air
Eye wall
Ey
Storm rotation
CLOCKWISE

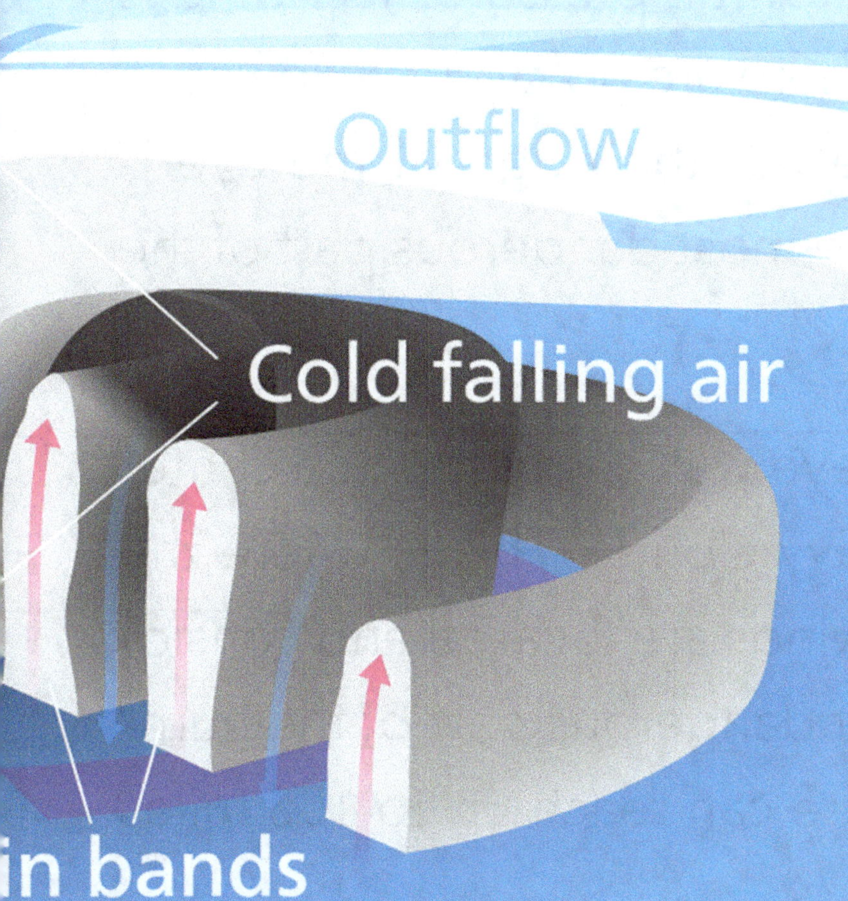
RUCTURE
EMISPHERE
Outflow
Cold falling air
in bands

PARTS OF A HURRICANE EYE

EYE – The eye is located at the center of a hurricane consisting of low air pressure. The wind is typically calm and there are no clouds. However, the eye wall, located at the edge of the eye is considered to be the most dangerous part of the hurricane.

EYE WALL – The eye wall surrounds the center and consists of heavy clouds. This is where the highest speeds of winds are located and considered to be the most dangerous part of the hurricane. The winds here can reach up to 155 miles per hour.

RAINBANDS – Large spirally bands of rain are known as rainbands. These can drop a great amount of rainfall that causes flooding as it hits land.

DIAMETER - Hurricanes are able to turn into huge storms. Its diameter measures from one side to the other and scan span more than 600 miles.

HEIGHT - The storm clouds powering the hurricanes can be very tall and reach up to nine miles in the atmosphere.

WHEN DO HURRICANES OCCUR?

Hurricane Season in the Caribbean and Atlantic Ocean occurs between June 1st and November 30th of each year.

WHY ARE HURRICANES DANGEROUS?

As they hit land, they are able to cause a great amount of damage. Most of it results from flooding and storm surges. They can also cause wind damage, blowing down trees and damaging homes. Hurricanes can also sometimes create small tornadoes.

Morning after Super Typhoon Yolanda/Haiyan hits Panay island in the Philippines.

WHERE DO THE NAMES COME FROM?

The names of hurricanes that form in the Atlantic come from a list maintained by the World Meteorological Organization. They are named in alphabetical order and named as they occur. They retain six lists of these names and each year they use a new list.

Hurricane Isabel, 18 September 2003.

CATEGORIES

TROPICAL CYCLONES are defined in accordance with the speed of their sustained winds.

A **TROPICAL DEPRESSION** occurs when winds are 38 mph or less.

A **TROPICAL STORM** occurs when the winds range from 39 to 73 mph.

A **CATEGORY 1** Hurricane occurs when the winds range from 74 to 95 mph.

A **CATEGORY 2** Hurricane occurs when the winds range from 96 to 110 mph.

A **CATEGORY 3** Hurricane occurs when the winds range from 111 to 129 mph.

A **CATEGORY 4** Hurricane occurs when the winds range from 130 to 156 mph.

A **CATEGORY 5** Hurricane occurs when the winds reach 157 or higher mph.

Tornado over a dusty field.

TORNADOES

Tornadoes consist of violent columns of wind spinning very fast. They come from the bottom of a thunderstorm to the ground, having winds as fast as 300 miles per hour. They are smaller than the hurricanes are and form over land. They obtain their energy from thunderstorms. Water-spouts are tornadoes forming over water. Prior to a tornado touching ground, it is referred to as a funnel cloud.

Beautifully structured supercell thunderstorm in American Plains.

HOW DO TORNADOES FORM?

During discussion regarding tornadoes, people generally talk about the large tornadoes occurring during a thunderstorm. These tornadoes will form tall clouds known as cumulonimbus clouds. However, there are other conditions that need to take place in order for a tornado to occur.

These steps typically have to occur for the formation of a tornado:

- A huge thunderstorm takes place within a cumulonimbus cloud.

- The wind has to change direction with a wind speed at high altitude causing the air to swirl horizontally.

- Air rises from the ground to push up onto the swirling air to tip it over.

- The funnel of swirling air sucks more warm air up from the ground.

- This funnel then gets longer, stretching to the ground.

- Once it touches the ground it then becomes a tornado.

A very rare Funnel Cloud from a passing storm cell over Arlington Arizona in December 2014.

TORNADO CHARACTERISTICS

SHAPE – They will typically appear as a thin funnel coming from the clouds to the ground. Occasionally, a giant tornado may appear to be shaped more like a wedge.

SIZE – They vary greatly in size. In the United States, a tornado is typically around 500 feet across, but some are very narrow and some can be almost two miles wide.

WIND SPEED – Its wind speed varies from 65 up to 250 miles per hour.

WIND SPEED – Its wind speed varies from 65 up to 250 miles per hour.

COLOR – Tornadoes appear in various colors, dependent on the local environment. Some appear to be almost invisible, and others can be gray, white, black, red, blue, and even green.

ROTATION – In the northern hemisphere, most rotate counter-clockwise while the tornadoes in the southern hemisphere rotate clockwise.

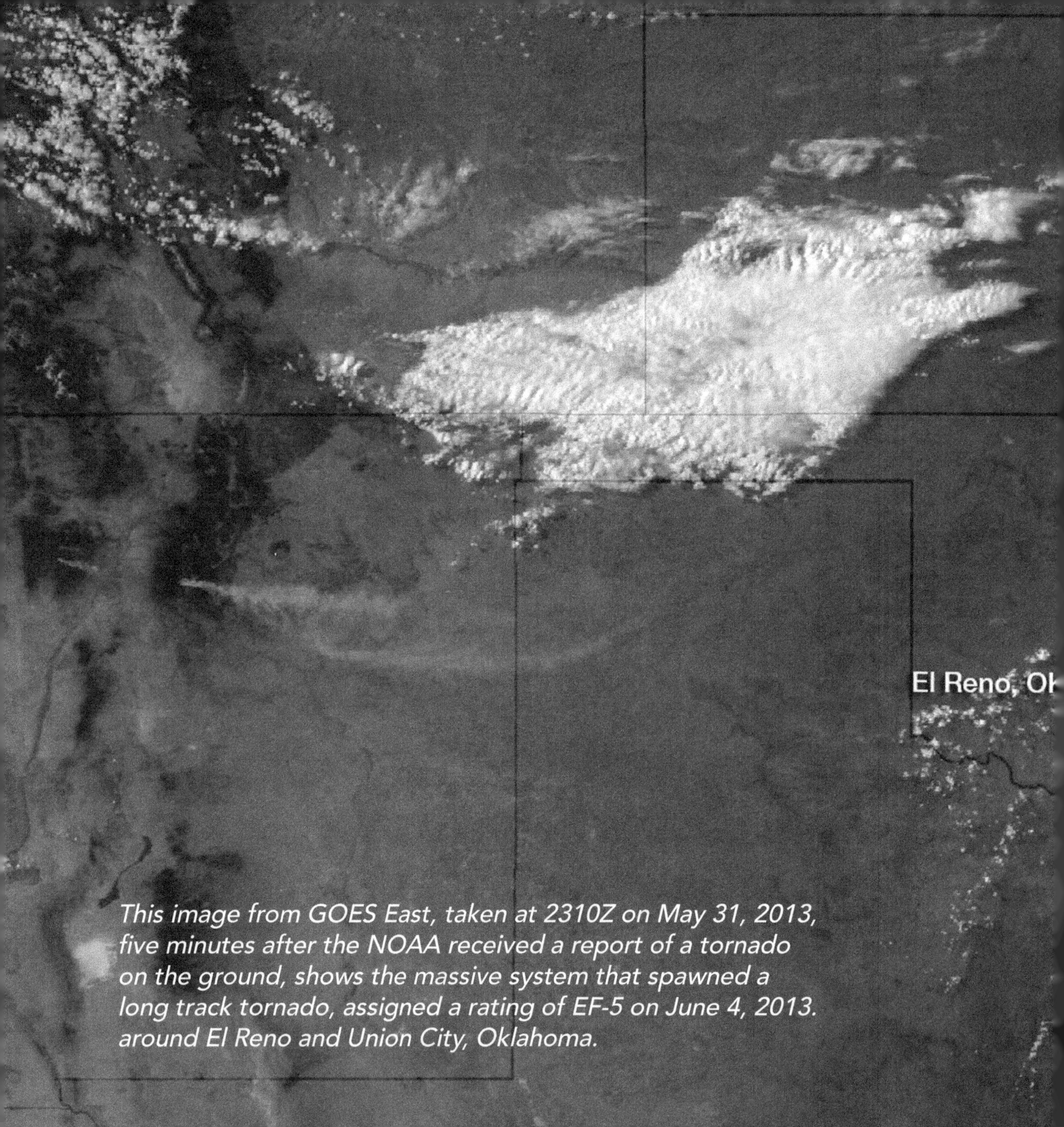

El Reno, Ok
This image from GOES East, taken at 2310Z on May 31, 2013,
five minutes after the NOAA received a report of a tornado
on the ground, shows the massive system that spawned a
long track tornado, assigned a rating of EF-5 on June 4, 2013.
around El Reno and Union City, Oklahoma.

DIFFERENT TYPES OF TORNADOES

SUPERCELL – This is a long-lived, large thunderstorm and is known to produce some of the largest and more violent tornadoes.

Supercell storm.

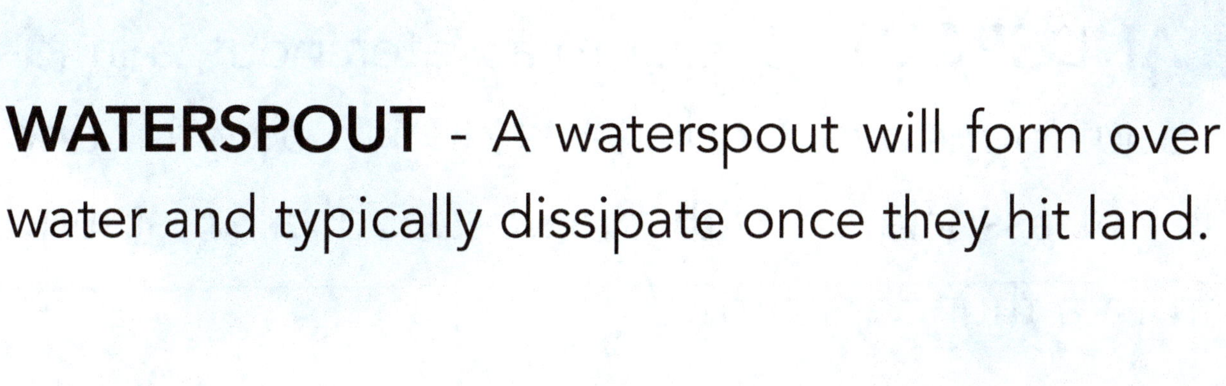

WATERSPOUT - A waterspout will form over water and typically dissipate once they hit land.

Spectacular waterspout over the sea.

LANDSPOUT - Similar to a waterspout, a landspout forms over land. It is known to be weak and is not associated with the vortex of air resulting from a thunderstorm.

GUSTNADO – A gustnado is known as a small tornado that forms during a weather front with gusts of wind.

A gustnado

MULTIPLE VORTEX - A multiple vortex is a tornado consisting of more than one spinning tubes of air.

Tornado.

CATEGORIES

The wind speed and amount of resulting damage is how tornadoes are categorized. The scale used is called the **"Enhanced Fujita"** scale, sometimes referred to as the "EF" scale.

- An **EF-O** tornado has a wind speed strength of 65-85 miles per hour, and is considered weak.

- An **EF-1** tornado has wind speeds from 86-110 miles per hour and is also considered weak.

- An **EF-2** tornado has wind speeds of 111-135 miles per hour and is considered strong.

- An **EF-3** tornado has wind speeds of 136-165 miles per hours and is considered strong.

- An **EF-4** tornado has wind speeds between 166-200 miles per hour and considered violent.

- An **EF-5** tornado has wind speeds over 200 miles per hour and considered violent.

Supercell near Vega, Texas - May 2012.

WHERE DO THEY MOSTLY OCCUR?

Tornadoes are able to form almost anywhere, but in the United States, most of them occur in Tornado Alley. This area goes from north Texas to South Dakota and from Missouri to the Rocky Mountains.

TORNADO WARNINGS AND WATCHES

While storms can be fascinating to watch, they can also be very dangerous. Be sure to stay inside and close to your parents, doing exactly as they say.

For additional information on extreme weather you can go to your local library, research the internet, or ask questions of your teachers, parents, and friends.

Visit

BABY PROFESSOR
EDUCATION KIDS

www.BabyProfessorBooks.com
to download Free Baby Professor eBooks
and view our catalog of new and exciting
Children's Books